Jamie Drake's

New American
GLAMOUR

Jamie Drake's

New American
GLAMOUR

Principal photography by William Waldron

BULFINCH PRESS
New York · Boston

Bulfinch Press

Time Warner Book Group

1271 Avenue of the Americas, New York, NY 10020

Visit our Web site at www.bulfinchpress.com

First Edition: October 2005

Library of Congress Cataloging-in-Publication Data

Drake, Jamie.
    Jamie Drake's new American glamour / Jamie Drake.
        p. cm.
Includes index.
ISBN 0-8212-5716-1
    1. Drake, Jamie. 2. Interior decoration — United States. I. Title:
    New American glamour. II. Title.
NK2004.3D737 A4 2005
747'.092 — dc22

                                                    2005000225

Designed by Lisa Vaughn-Soraghan, Two of Cups Design Studio

PRINTED IN SINGAPORE

For
Meryl and Lester . . . always
Jason . . . now and forever

Introduction.

As one eighteenth-century poet, Allan Ramsay, put it, "When devils, wizards or jugglers deceive the sight, they are said to cast glamour o'er the eyes of the spectator." Of course, that's far easier said than done.

008

Glamour is a way of life. It's also a style of interior design, and I think a particularly American style. What I call the New American Glamour derives in part from the old MGM motto: "Make it big! Do it right! Give it class!" These interiors — my interiors — are confident, bold, and polished. They're assertive but not overbearing. They reveal themselves in a gesture, through posture and movement. They incorporate sunshine and hope and passion and stylish certainty. They have a "look at me, world, here I am" attitude. Of course, the New American Glamour also describes my clients: self-made, assured people who have accomplished remarkable things and who want interiors that reflect their intellect, their vivacity, their appetite for life. Fortunately for us, America in the twenty-first century gives us access to the absolute best of everything.

I have always been aware of glamour. Certainly its surface shimmer captivates my earliest memories. From age three or so, I know I was conscious of the cut of my mother's dress, of

I have loved these Gene Davis silk-screened stripes since I was a child, and I know that they have influenced the way that I see color — that it transforms, surprises, and lies. This amazing nineteenth-century English glass candlestick, for example, is a shade of purple so deep that it reads as black in any light, but blacker still surrounded by saturated hues.

the chiffon drape of a décolletage on a cocktail dress emphasized by a sparkling brooch, of high heels, of scents and perfume, of bizarrely over-the-top printed wallpapers, of big, blowsy cabbage roses, and of a dining room papered in an *empire en grisaille* taupe, black, and white wallpaper, and of French provincial furniture glinting, as it were, from the dull burnish of the gilt hardware.

My first real taste of American glamour came, however, with the discovery of a junk pile behind my childhood best friend's house in Woodbridge, Connecticut. Abutting a decrepit barn and an abandoned farmhouse, this trove of treasures yielded loads of old crockery and broken glass bottles, all the sorts of cast-off things that, at age five or six, I thought were antiques. My friend Larry and I would drag our pickings off to the fort that we were building. Even at that age I was in charge of decorating and antiques. As I remember, we built the fort in a sort of natural pit. We had moved some big rocks to create a ring of boulders, and I think we worked on the edges to form a curved banquette — very Palm Springs,

Arthur Elrod, 1965, Rat Pack–cool. I can recall working diligently to get the composition of a discarded zinc washbasin and a collection of old bottles just right, setting the basin on its side next to the bottles, which I arranged according to height.

I'm grateful that my parents encouraged me so whole-heartedly in all my creative endeavors. My mother was a painter (she trained at the Yale Art School) and my father was in the printing business, as was his father, in New Haven. One of my earliest memories involves accompanying my father to his paper warehouse, where it was wonderfully chilly, and smelled deliciously of paper. I found the printing presses completely captivating, and the perfume of ink that permeated the plant was to me quite irresistible — as were, of course, the viscous, shiny, oily inks themselves, the mixing process, and the way the color separators managed to get each hue of the rainbow exactly right.

A few years later, I began drawing elaborate house plans and complicated game boards (my own version of Monopoly,

[above and opposite, bottom] I recently came across a trove of my early drawings, which my parents had saved for all these years. I was flabbergasted to see how closely my adult work parallels the fantasias of my childhood in terms of color, luster, and the repetition of form.

[opposite, top] I've used transparent bubbles of glass, mirror, and iridescence to add sparkle, shine, and glitter since I was a teenager. Clearly, the glamour of luster, reflection, and light struck me early and has never dissipated. So, apparently, did the desire to arrange rooms into comfortable conversation areas, to spice up a sectional sofa with multicolored throw pillows, to use bold geometric patterns on the wall.

Chutes and Ladders, and the Game of Life). Not long ago I unearthed a stack of those drawings of room interiors, and I was staggered to see that I've never changed my leopard spots! The full-fantasy Technicolor eclecticism that I reveled in then, on the backs of the cardboards from my father's shirts, so closely resembles my palettes and my preferences today that it's almost eerie.

By the time I was eight or nine, and devouring every shelter and fashion magazine I could get my hands on, I knew that I wanted to be an interior designer — or decorator, or whatever it was called then. Two of my father's first cousins were very well-known designers: Yale Burge, in New York City, and his brother, Bernard Burge, who was probably

Connecticut's most prestigious residential designer and who had the most fabulous treasure trove of a shop. To this day his apartment epitomizes chic for me. I must have seen it for the last time as a child, but my memory of it is seminal and exceptionally vivid. The drawing room was a very sophisticated and contemporary interpretation of *grisaille*: every piece of furniture was upholstered in the same gray-and-white fabric, one of those fresh, almost naïve, somewhat muted Matissey patterns that Billy Baldwin had designed for Woodson. The throw pillows added the only shocks of color, a brilliant coral orange.

We moved into the house where I spent most of my childhood — and which Bernie decorated — when I was four. Seven or eight years later, my mother decided not only that it was time to redecorate, but that she and I would do it together. Most of the house sang with color: vibrant raspberry-magenta wall covering in the breakfast room and kitchen and luscious orange tones elsewhere. But when it came to my room, I was adamant: black patent leather with white lacquered moldings was the only décor that interested me. My mother absolutely hated the idea. But I was a diabolical child, and I wanted this black room, so I said: "It's black or nothing."

I got my way. For a bedspread I commandeered some antique black-and-white toile de Jouy that my mother had had made into a banquet cloth. I placed the bed on a 45-degree angle out of the corner of the room, and against it I set an old table that I sprayed with white lacquer. Then I began cultivating my flower-arranging skills, traipsing into the woods regularly to discover which flowers, plants, and weeds would thrive in a vase, and which ones wilted within the hour. And the black patent leather stayed until my parents sold the house.

Vibrant color appeals to me at all times of the day, in all types of rooms. The rather eclectic but boldly colored design of this breakfast area, with its hand-combed walls and calculatedly mismatched chairs, may hark back to the raspberry room where my family gathered each morning.

I habitually plundered my father's printing plant for great materials to work with at home: paper to draw on and metal lithography plates that I would cut and pound and stamp to use for my macramé creations, which turned into my first real business. I took up macramé with an absolute passion in my early teens, knotting away the nights in front of the television, dragging my mother day after day to every Caldor's and hardware store in the area in search of twines of different textures and thicknesses — from marvelous thin white nylon cords to big heavy ropes in various colors, all of which I tied and manipulated with the objects I created from those metal plates and other baubles.

I made masses of things, some of them quite rustic. But there were also a lot of very delicate things, bibs and vests with fringe to the floor, made from extremely fine gauge cotton and the nylon threads that I liked to think were silk. I used to add cheap silvered and gilded Christmas ornaments for texture, sparkle, and shine; some of them I boiled until the silver flaked off, leaving just transparent bubbles of glass. They glistened so lustrously, so fragilely, so elusively in that gossamer fringe. Almost every weekend for several years my mother or father would drive me to one craft show or another. I'd set up my display of handcrafted macramé and sit there for a day or sometimes two and — especially at the height of the holiday shopping season — come home with five or six hundred dollars. What a kick to learn that a creative outlet could also be lucrative.

By my midteens I had started focusing on interior design quite seriously. Fortunately for me, there was a regional public arts high school in New Haven. The administration arranged an apprenticeship at what was then Connecticut's leading contract interiors firm. For my last year and a half of school I spent half days there, five days a week — and full time in the summer.

That experience taught me one of the fundamental principles that every designer should take to heart: adaptability. I am passionate about the choices I make for a project, but never a slave to them. There is always another way to combine the volume of resource options, so one's choices need never be limited. I also began to learn the basic tools of design: drafting skills, for example, afford you enormous flexibility in solving problems and laying out furniture arrangements — not, of course, that I knew how to draft then. I also realized, moreover, that if you're interested in the latest trends, as I am and certainly was then, the influx of innovative materials, the plastics and resins and metal treatments and alloys, is constant and always arrives at the contract side of the business first. Another winning aspect of the experience was realizing just how wonderful it can be to work in a collegial atmosphere. I still am close with the person who supervised me there — he seemed ancient to me at the time, but he was probably just a few years out of college himself.

Immediately after graduation from high school, I enrolled at Parsons School of Design, class of 1975. At that time, Parsons had what it called the Environmental Design Department. The curriculum addressed every type of design challenge, from products to buildings, graphics, landscapes, and interiors, as compared to a more traditional approach of singular specialties. They taught us how to think about modeling space, about balance, scale, and form. They taught us how to problem solve, and about innovation. They couldn't have cared less whether chintz goes with damask or where to get the best silk velvet. Color theory was a must, as was the history of architecture, but the history of furniture you had to learn on your own — thank heavens for all those childhood

Nature may abhor a vacuum, but she certainly adores the repetition of form, as do I. In this tablescape, I explored the curve, the circle, and the sphere in as many man-made and homegrown permutations as possible.

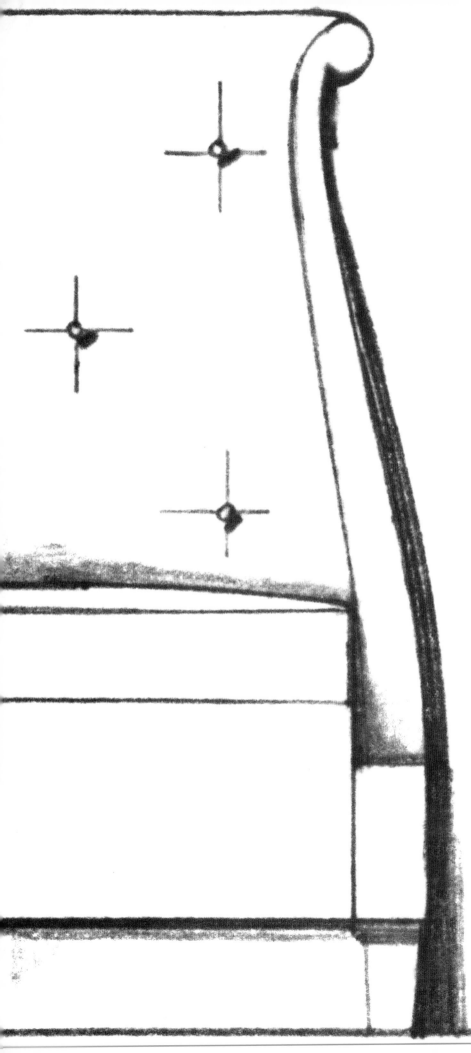

trips to the Wadsworth Athenaeum in Hartford, as well as the study rooms at the Metropolitan Museum of Art and the Brooklyn Museum, to say nothing of New York City's other extraordinary resources.

Parsons may not have always been the most supportive environment for those, like me, with a highly decorative bent (I was certainly hell-bent on finishing in three years, rather than the standard four), but it was a terrific place to profit from your mistakes, if you chose to do so — as one project in particular proved to me. The hypothetical client was a couple returning to the city, empty nesters, who had bought a brownstone floor-through. The functional program specified what they needed in terms of living spaces and storage requirements, and gave us information about how the clients entertained. There was one aesthetic requirement, and only one: the clients' collection of antique farm implements had to be included in the design.

My solution consisted of draping the entire master bedroom in platinum silk satin. For the floor I designed a polka-dotted rug of wool, silk, and Lurex — cream-colored background, lavender and deep purple dots with gold Lurex halos — atop a platinum-gray wool carpet. An enormous Boulle desk sat against one wall. Over it hung the farm implements, drawn quite beautifully. I dressed to suit the occasion, or so I thought: skin-tight cream-colored jeans, gold Fiorucci boots, a lavender cashmere cowl-neck sweater with a saucy scarf wrapped around my neck à la Française, and a gold Mylar belt just to set it all off.

When I'd finished my presentation, the panel of teachers said, "Well, we don't quite know where to look first — at your presentation or at your outfit. We don't think that's a good thing." Thankfully, they gave me an opportunity to redo it. In the course of the revision process Lou Goodman, one of my favorite teachers, said something that I remember to this day about looking at history and learning from it, and then reinterpreting it — which I guess was related to our history of architecture course, where *Learning from Las Vegas*, by Robert Venturi, Stephen Izenour, and Denise Scott Brown, was the read of the moment. Lou referred specifically to Versailles, and to the architectural device of the enfilade (a series of rooms opening "in file" one to the next), which is what a successful solution to this hypothetical required. I realized that I needed a different vocabulary, and in the process of developing one I discovered how to redo the apartment in a way that was still me, but that made sense to my professors. Maybe the experience taught me about being flexible and more than a little something about what it takes to excel. At any rate, I still have both versions of that project in my archives.

While I was still in college I interned one summer at Angelo Donghia's office, spending most of my time at the drafting board working on elevations of the bathrooms and kitchen in the late designer's famous octagonal house in Key West. Drafting was never my strong suit, and I remember him pointing out that I had elevated things upside down and backwards. I also slaved over drawings for his first foray into production furniture — a mass-market collection for a company called Kroehler, now long out of business. My drawings were based on his sketches and marvelous pictures that he'd taken in China of some 1930s hotel chairs and other things. A hush hung over that office. The quiet taught me about the glamour that exists in presenting your work to a client in a serious, professional manner, so that they respect and honor the effort that you put in and thus, I guess, the bills that accrue because of it.

I started my business literally, quite literally, two days after graduation, more by a chance phone call and felicity than by grand plan. A friend asked if I would be interested in doing apartments for her boyfriend and her boyfriend's father, both of whom had decided to move at the same time into the same building on Fifth Avenue. They sent a car to whisk me up to Greenwich for a barbecue and a chat: my first

[above] I designed this chair for the Kips Bay Showhouse a few years ago. It was inspired by a seventeenth-century tall-back chair and uses thick, twisted rope for the arms, ending in a tasseled flourish.

[opposite] Most designers prefer, whenever possible, to design furnishings for specific clients. But the process is not an easy one, and mastering the form of a chair may be among the most difficult tasks that any designer encounters. Chairs are sculpture, but sculpture that must fit the body. This design is from my latest furniture collection.

two projects essentially fell into my lap. A third, on Sutton Place, came later that summer, and more followed simply by word of mouth. A number of referrals came from the placement director at Parsons, who would get calls from people saying something like, "Gee, we have a house we want to design and decorate, but we thought we'd like to have somebody who's new and fresh." These clients weren't necessarily searching for a bargain. In fact, many of the projects had what at the time were considered rather large budgets. At that point, I didn't have any completed work to show them, just my portfolio of school drawings, which, even in retrospect, still amazes me.

Nothing could be more obvious from those student efforts, much less from the interiors I fashioned on my father's shirt

[above] This lush tabletop close-up exemplifies my love of the Midas touch. The French porcelain has wide gold borders, as does the antique cut-crystal stemware.

[opposite] Large scale equals big glamour. A superb gilt bronze chandelier circa 1860 is the enormous central feature of this reception hall. The Andy Warhol painting in the background hangs above a Henry Moore sculpture, creating a glittering tableau, bracketed by a pair of gilt bronze sconces.

cardboards, than my own certainty about the sort of world that I've always wanted to inhabit. That world delights in color and revels in the joys of form and texture. It loves luster. It celebrates diversity: the more expansive the mix, the better.

Beige on beige on beige is not for me. I like brightness and vivacity, and more than a little touch of Midas. I like things to gleam and reflect off one another. Color and luster move your eye throughout the room. Yet it's more complicated than that: dissect my projects and you'll find that the rooms really are, in fact, quite neutral. Strong color endows each space with a thrill — and a treat. Luster makes the light dance around the interior.

Form, like texture, elicits the tactile desires. I'm especially attracted to the circle and to its sibling, the curve. Repeating a

Strong color endows each space with a thrill — and a treat. Luster makes the light dance around the interior.

family of forms throughout a room helps to activate the space — to make the planes come alive. While I generally prefer to exercise my formula for form through the voluptuousness of the curve, the device of repetition applies to all types of geometry — the square, the triangle, the hexagon, the octagon, the rectangle.

Complexity attracts and holds your interest in a room. In fact, I think that complexity ultimately provides the key to why clients seek out designers. Most clients want their residences tailored to them. They're looking for the perfect fit, for rooms that reflect the variety of their life experiences, their dreams, their interests, their family histories. We're required to put together incredibly diverse things, things gathered on travels far and wide, things from cultures that have nothing in common except that each cultivates its distinctive heritage of art and craft.

Exoticism has always been compelling, because it's an adventure of sorts into the unknown. From Chinese lacquer and animal prints to the exuberant ornament, riotous colors, and perfected hand-skills of Asia, the Near East, and North Africa, there's nothing like the glamour of a previously unexperienced three-dimensional reality. Variety is as infinite as the capacity of human imagination. It may be intimidating. It's always exhilarating.

On the pillow: GUESTS OF GUESTS MAY NOT BRING GUESTS

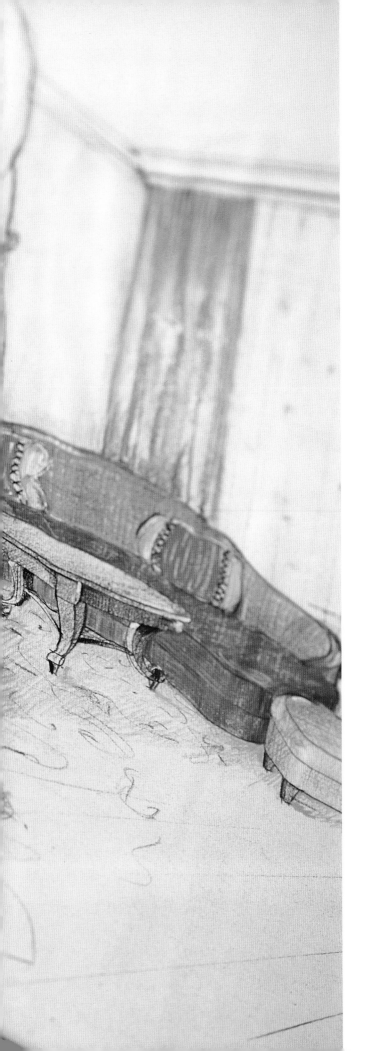

I have always been aware of glamour. Certainly its surface shimmer captivates my earliest memories.

For me, iridescent things are inherently glamorous. Tar, buckets of printer's ink, cans full of paint, a spill of oil — each is thick and luscious. They move, and their viscosity is inseparable from the shine that has the power to transform, to make the light dance across a surface, to make the surface metamorphose into something else right before your eyes. That's a very special kind of wizardry, and we experience it every sunny day when we walk down a sidewalk that looks like it's paved with diamond dust.

Interior design continually tests our capacity for invention. It also offers the possibility of living in a party moment all the time. What could be more glamorous than living out a dream, especially the American dream? What is more exciting than having a fantasy about a space and bringing it to life? What beats recreating the memory of a perfect moment in order to make it last a little longer — even, perhaps, for a very long time? Interior design at its best and at its most American celebrates the infinite wonder of life and the constant potential for progress. There is nothing more glamorous than that.

Luster.

L uster is glamour at its most active. It gleams. It glows. It glimmers and glistens. It shimmers and shines and sparkles. Luster compels light to dance around a room, which is a bit of wizardry in and of itself. What, after all, is more magical than a reflection — or a shot of radiance in the dark?

I'm very attracted to spaces that have a certain kind of evocative atmosphere, spaces that are textured with pools of **light** and areas of shadow. I tend to create that kind of atmosphere by using a lower light level than many other designers, which is why luster is an absolute imperative for me. In a room where the light is in diminuendo, flattering as that lower light level may be, anything that shines, however subtly, contributes a necessary degree of illumination. I think that's why I love glazed porcelains, silk satins, Murano glass chandeliers, gilt bronze, and nickled silver, among other things. I know that's why I love swaths of silk at the window: they add **sheen** and shadow to the wall surface of a room lit by a 25-watt bulb and three candles. They catch the light. They flicker.

Just as with color, I choreo- graph luster throughout the room to ensure that there are no dead zones. If you set something glimmering in each corner and maybe something gleaming in the center of the room, you create **glistening** pin- points throughout the space, and the eye keeps moving. Lustrous materials light each area subtly, from within. The materials can be

as fancily iridescent as mother of pearl or as quietly **gleaming** as the cabochon jewels and metal links that remind me of my favorite jewelry. But they can also be simple — say, inexpensive glass votive candles made by Alpha Workshops wrapped in gunmetal chain, which glisten on the exterior, glow from within, and just plain sparkle. The effects can range from the high reflectivity of mirror and lacquer to the softer sheen of **pearlized** top coats, of cotton and wool fabrics woven with metallic leatherette, of screening materials woven out of metal and metal meshes. The luster of natural silk is both alpha and omega in my vocabulary, from the low-luster slubbiness of raw silk to the high-polish sheen of silk satin. Moreover, combining levels of contrasting lusters — such as satin piping, welting, and buttons against a more light-absorbent matte fabric — often elicits considerable pleasure for the eye.

Luster generates a bit of mystery about where the perimeters are or how sharp an edge may be. **Iridescent** surfaces change their appearance depending on the perspective of the viewer and the quality of the ambient and accent lighting, which is why luster on the walls can be so enormously effective, whether you achieve it with pearlescent paint finishes or, more theatrically, with Mylar papers or mirrors. Consider those marvelous, almost insanely reflect- ive rooms from the 1970s, the ones that seemed to be paneled entirely in strips of beveled **mirror**. The corridors, for example, were modern halls of mirror — as were the elevator lobbies and building foyers — and they still do a little disco dance in my imagination even though they're completely passé now. Valerian Rybar's work was silvered aplenty, with mirrored strips and stainless-steel waffle patterns; Jay Spectre's corrugated steel bedroom seemed both hard and soft at the same time.

Mirrors are classic, and they needn't always be totally clear or totally **reflective**. In fact, they can be as blatant or as mysterious as you choose: an unblemished mirror provides a perfect reflection; peach mirror creates a soft romance; sandblasted mirror blurs appealingly; antiqued mirror adds an appealing patina of age. You can use mercury mirror, which is itself something of a delightful conundrum: very old-fashioned but also very modernist, with a surface quality that's almost liquid, like water that's been poured behind a sheet of glass and that reflects light — and anything else — abstractly, seductively, amorphously.

A dining room is the perfect place to play up the aspects of luster. For one client we installed brilliant Chinese red and bright coral-orange taffeta curtains layered on top of sheers that are beaded all over with tiny individual caviar beads that catch the candlelight and **sparkle** wonderfully in the glow of the chandelier. The luster appears in the high polish of the giant mahogany table. A set of twenty-four antique English rosewood chairs covered in silk velvet adds elements of sheen; the silk cord outlining the shape and form of the chairs lends highlights. The gilt bronze and **crystal** of the chandelier provides luster and sparkle overhead.

When I first graduated from Parsons I tried to play by the rules and was extremely rigid on the matter of mixing metals — among other no-nos. A room had to be all brass, or all chrome. At that point, of course, the tastes of the era dictated a few choices and were limited to just brass or just chrome, buffed to the highest possible **polish**. As my work has evolved — as I've evolved — I've allowed myself more freedom to break those boring rules.

Severing the bonds of those pressing preconceptions about so-called tastefulness affords you a kind of luxurious liberty to make the gestures and flourishes that create rooms of interest and complexity. I began to find that assuredness as my career developed and I began working on projects that involved more and more antiques. As you learn to value each and every object for its own individual beauty, however idiosyncratic, you start to develop the means to incorporate numerous distinctive pieces into a harmonious scheme, and you no longer penalize the dissenter for being of a different tonality, say, than the base metal that you used to smelt the majority of the room.

Luster may be the one quality that all of us associate with the glory that is the glamour of Hollywood, and with its remarkable faces and fictions, especially those of the 1930s. Dapper and debonair, soigné and sophisticated, evanescent and eternal, such are the forms and figures that flicker on the silver screen. Those images contain, for me, the essence of urbanity and glamour. So do the sparkle and **twinkle** of the lights on our skyscrapers, and that's what I try to bring indoors.

029

Luster may be the one quality that all of us associate with the glory that is the glamour of Hollywood, and with its remarkable faces and fictions, especially those of the 1930s.

There are so many different degrees and types of luster, and an almost infinite selection of lustrous surfaces. Here I combined high-gloss lacquer and highly polished stone with low-sheen woods, highly reflective metal accents, and a range of refractive surfaces at all different levels to choreograph the way light moves through, up, and around the interior. Little details include the sofa's mirrored legs; the pillows' lustrous sheen; the table base's polished brass accents.

For me, Fred Astaire and Ginger Rogers epitomize American glamour. I want each room I design to radiate something of the essence and spirit of that incomparable duo, to trip its own light fantastic. Every room should have its own grace, wit, and style of motion, but every room should also do the Continental, as it were. That requires luster, because it is luster that makes the light, and hence the eye and the heart, dance.

Combining lustrous objects and elements from different times and places in the same space poses a fascinating challenge: how do you layer luster upon luster? It takes a Midas touch. Each object is alight not only because of its gleaming finish, but also because of the aura of its history and culture and material technique. Japanese lacquer contains gold dust. The colors of Chinese, Korean, and Vietnamese lacquers have an almost infinite depth. There's the liquid quality of an antique polished mahogany, the gleam of polished silver, the golden glance of a gilded frame under a picture light.

One of the fantastic things about luster is that it actually softens a room, so that even hard surfaces seem to lose their edge. Because the light reflects as you move around the interior, it blurs the perimeters of a space. Light can also appear to dissolve the outlines of any form that is sheathed in a shining, lustrous skin; it can make something solid appear almost liquid, like the highly polished top of this mahogany dining table, which is also edged in gilt.

I like to use luster — particularly subtle luster — to add texture, and even pattern, to a room. Here, the grander gleaming gestures involve gilt, silver, crystal, polished stone, and highly polished mahogany. But the sheers at the window have just a hint of glitter, too: hand-detailed with caviar beads, they quietly add the barest note of shimmer to that side of the room.

The gilt bronze and crystal of the chande-lier provides luster and sparkle overhead.

Haute couture is one of the most glamorous things I know. It glorifies handwork at its most intricate, like the embroideries of Lesage or Holland & Sherry. Every designer dreams about bringing that level of handcraft to a room. Sometimes we can: these hand-beaded sheers sparkle next to a Russian urn with gilt bronze mounts.

I'm attracted to all of the materials that shine or glitter or sparkle or gleam or reflect light around the room. In fact, they are the reason that I can create rooms with the lower light levels that I find so glamorous and flattering.

When it comes to luster, however, I prefer not to gild the lily — although I'm not sure that there can ever be too much of a good thing. Take this antique marble mantelpiece, for example. A soft glow emanates from the polished stone, heightened by just the right amount of gilded detail.

Inlay can supercharge already lively surfaces to the point of song and dance, particularly when the bits and pieces of the colorful composition are themselves highly polished or iridescent. This extraordinary nineteenth-century English sideboard, with its ebonized finish, polished granite top, fantastically fruity pattern of semiprecious stones, and gilded mounts, actually seems to shimmy in the light that reflects in different intensities off its various surfaces. The Chinese pottery horses, though posed at a prance, actually settle the eye down by giving it a rest in the rhythm of glancing gleam.

When I use crystal, I tend to use it selectively and only in certain situations. Of course, there's nothing more glamorous than the crystal drops and bobeches of a fabulous chandelier, but I think that the glamour that luster imparts to a room, and to an overall design scheme, can be applied delicately, and in layers — not just with the hard knock on the head that is the cumulative effect of masses of crystal.

Just as with color, I choreograph luster throughout the room to ensure that there are no dead zones.

Luster compels light to dance around a room, which is a bit of wizardry in and of itself.

While we often use traditional framed mirrors on the wall, we rarely mirror entire wall surfaces anymore. I remember the wonderful rooms of the 1970s, paneled entirely with beveled six-inch strips — although a better parallel here might be to the 1860s, when Jules Hardouin-Mansart added the Hall of Mirrors to Versailles. Who knows? The time may be ripe to revive the mirror-paneled room.

When it comes to furniture, Chippendale works a room like no other. Basking in the spotlight under the glorious sconces on this mirrored landing is an extraordinary ten-foot George III sofa, made about 1760 in the Chippendale workshop.

Art adds gloss to every residence. Some objects in this home — such as the maquette of Lady Liberty — reflect their owner's pride in being a citizen of New York.

Disco lives! To create a cabaret-style party room at home, I borrowed Sir John Soane's device of hand-blown convex mirrors, placing parabolic mirrors in the moldings in lieu of the classic mirrored ball. Backlit bookcases change colors at the flip of a switch, creating a wonderful patchwork of tinted light.

Other lustrous elements include Venetian plaster walls, silk taffeta upholstery on the banquette, matching curtains layered with silver linen gauze, and satin moiré striped table skirts. A Léger ceramic hangs over the fireplace, a diminutive Archipenko odalisque reclines on the mantel, and a Calder mobile flies overhead. [previous pages]

Gold is always glamorous, but other metals and materials can be equally chic. In the powder room, white gold glass mosaic tiles provide a shimmering contrast to the dulled shine of the adjacent Venetian plaster walls. Marble floor moldings match the polished marble and nickel vanity base, which is topped by a scalloped antique basin. Silvered fittings are highly reflective, as are the Venetian glass mirror and the sharply faceted wall sconces.

Colored acrylic resin panels, wonderful in their translucency, envelop the shower wall, the vanity top, and the bath surround. A shimmering, glittering, gold shower curtain and walls the color of crème caramel enrich the delightfully high-cholesterol effect of the amber-colored acrylic. Green glass mosaic tiles ground the space.

If I really wanted to be fancy, I'd say that I'd found my inspiration for this bath in the Amber Room, the fabled Eighth Wonder of the World. After all, I adore all things Russian. But really, I just happen to love butterscotch and toffee — the candy, that is.

Every one of the surfaces is polished to an extremely high gloss, apart from the dyed woods. The porcelain tub rests on a highly polished lacquer platform in the middle of the terrazzo-covered floor. A glass side table with fluted and scalloped details provides a glamorous note of transparency.

What could be more appropriate in a fantasy space than this flamboyant pair of eighteenth-century gilded chairs? My early love for Boulle has never diminished, so I still find myself attracted to pieces, like this commode, that show off the extraordinary marquetry techniques which distinguish the art of the *ebeniste*.

It's always wonderful when you can truly let your imagination go wild. But it's even more exciting when you find the stuff that your dreams are made of. That's why it's as important to stay abreast of new materials and designs as it is to really master tradition and history. You generally need both to bring a fantasy to fruition. It's hard work, but it's worth it — especially when the effect looks right, and effortless.

When you're always looking for new ways to add layers of luster and, often, high contrast to a room, you learn how to manipulate the many moods of light. The highly reflective fabric on the living room lounge chairs, for example, is something new for us. Long panels of metal mesh fabric drape the windows; the fabric glistens at night but virtually dissolves in the daylight. A chocolate-colored Venetian plaster seems to swallow the walls.

Luster generates a bit of mystery about where the perimeters are or how sharp an edge may be.

Iridescent
surfaces change
their appearance
depending on the
perspective of the
viewer . . .

There may be no simple
definition of glamour,
but you always know it when you see
it — and it always involves luster.
What's more glamorous than lamé and
patent, sequins and gilt, fur and velvet,
satin, beads and jewels, parchment
and leather? Just think of the magical
pointillism of shagreen or the iridescent
dappled texture that mother-of-pearl
provides.

   Think how glamorous it is to create
a party moment at home every day.
That's what lighting is for. It's also why
luster matters so much. There's nothing
more enchanting than the spell cast by
a riot of crystal and color overhead, or
by the gleam of metal or glint of jewels
or glow of silk as they move around a
room. The wizardry is up to you. It's as
straightforward as putting your lights
on dimmers, lighting a few candles,
using a beautiful scent, and setting out
at least one perfect lily.

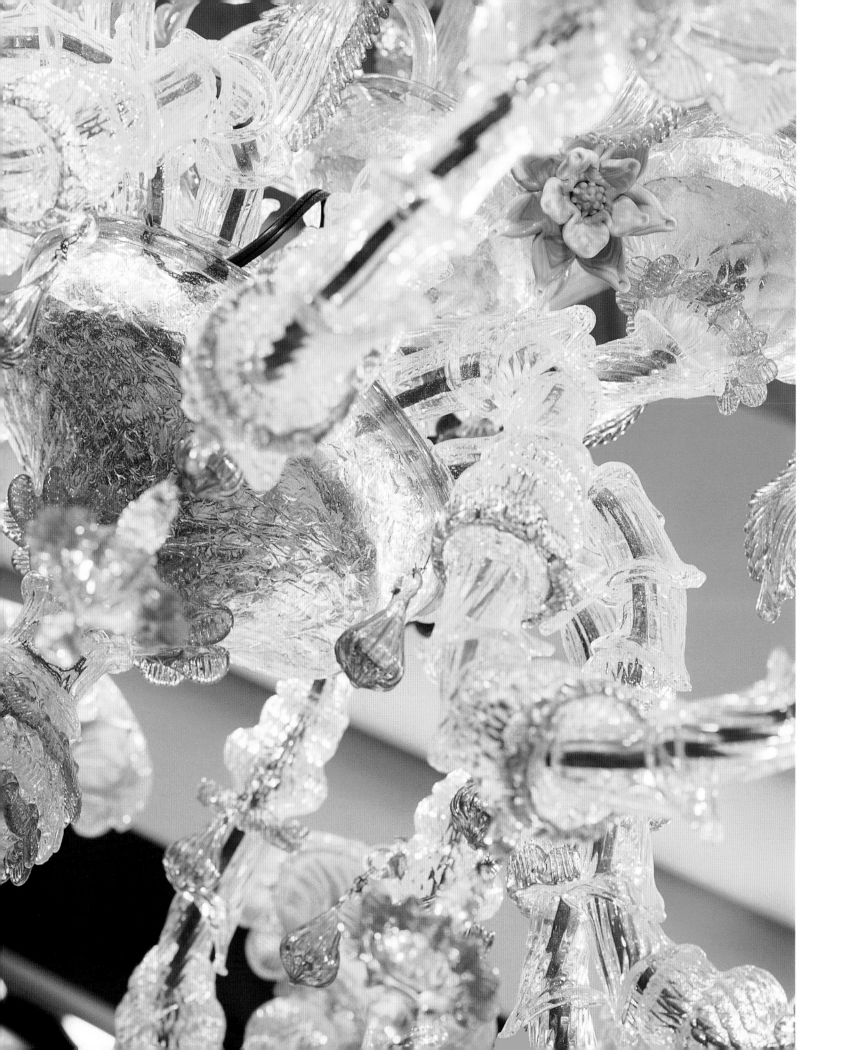

T he glamour of texture is the invitation to touch. If the curve elicits a come-hither call, surface texture sings a siren's song, especially for a designer like me, to whom variety and complexity matter so much. Because I tend to work mostly with solid colors — excepting, of course, my favorite stripes — I often use texture to create pattern. Luster contributes to that mix as well: the contrast of the highly reflective and lustrous with the much more matte forms a pattern of light and shadow. Color, texture, and luster are equal partners when it comes to endowing a room with enduring visual interest and **tactile** pleasure.

The four temperaments of texture are hard, soft, smooth, and rough. Each exists in endless variation, and the options are limitless, especially in the fascinating world of man-made materials. I'll often use texture in the same manner that I use color, manipulating one sort of surface, say, **chunky**, in a range of different grades and qualities — that is, small, smaller, and smallest chunks, some in a random arrangement, others in a highly organized group. I also love to play with textures in high contrast, exaggerating the interaction of rough with smooth or hard with soft, abutting the more **nubbly** against the seamless.

Texture can be far more than just an inducement for the eye to set the hand in motion. At its most evocative, texture creates a very

special kind of drama. The theater of materials offers a means of exploring the possible characters of surface and finish to the maximum. Texture is also a measure of age, a level of patina, a degree of refinement.

Fabrics and **finishes** may be the most obviously textural elements of any design, but furniture can lend some piquancy to the textural mélange as well. Consider case goods, for example. As far as I'm concerned, there's nothing less interesting than walking into a room that looks like a solid sea of brown, with the same dominant wood tone for end tables, coffee tables, consoles, nesting tables, bookshelves, frame chairs. Wood has innate texture and color and can be treated in innumerable different ways. It also, as we all know, reveals its age magnificently. So while it's wonderful to use wood in a room — you can hardly escape it, actually — it's more intriguing when the pieces don't match. I like to work with a range of species and a broad array of finishes, everything from stripped and **waxed** to marquetry and mirrors. Tables, after all, can be topped with all sorts of materials: marble, lacquer, *verre eglomise*, and gilt, for example, form a voluptuous mosaic of textures.

Animal skins, of course, have been glamorous textures forever, as have lamé, patent, jeweled, beaded, embroidered, and sequined surfaces, silks and velvets. But exotic skins infuse a room with pattern and texture, and it doesn't matter whether they are real, faux, printed, **woven**, silk velvet, or hand-hooked. Animal skins are inevitable, really, when you think of the role that they've played in the history of interiors. Percier et Fontaine enlivened the interiors of the Napoleonic era with those skin tones, as did Madeleine Castaing, Syrie Maugham, Lady Mendl, Sister Parish, and Albert Hadley. And let's not forget leather: dyed, brushed, gauffraged, suede, or stamped, leather has always been luxe, as has the plushness of all sorts of furs. That fascination with the refined and treated surface extends to shagreen, goatskin, parchment, and so on.

I'm currently using a lot of textiles that are woven with materials that radiate light. A favorite right now is a wool fabric that incorporates strands of silver metallic faux leather. I've recently discovered a particularly fetching fabric made of pieced calfskins stitched in little strips. While the pieces aren't large, they are quite precious and appear more so because of their diminutive size. Lately, I've upholstered all types of seating with it: seats of chairs and stools, as well as ottomans and other things, and I'd love to panel an entire room with it. You could apply each piece in a series of alternating stripes to create a parquet pattern. Wouldn't that be Jean-Michel Frank *jazzy*?

I couldn't live without my daily dose of *Women's Wear Daily*. Fashion, at least for me, is an endless font of inspiration for those delicious details that finish a room. So much of texture emerges from the dressmaker touches: the smocking on a lampshade, embroidery, beading, and buttons, the swag of a drape, the bed skirt with a thousand tiny pleats, the bouffant silk-taffeta bow straight from a Valentino dress. And then, of course, there's fringe, which takes me back to my teenage passion for macramé. What is an interlocking of knots if not an exploration of texture? I love the idea of that, and the challenge of creating something which has a gossamer quality but will last through a nuclear winter — or at least stand up to everyday wear and tear.

It takes time to develop a palette of textures. But it all begins with the client. My first challenge is to take a measure of who that individual is, how that person wants to present himself or herself to the world, how he or she wants to live, and how they will use the space that I'm designing — and it's completely intuitive on that level. The client generally provides me with some very helpful clues. As I feel my way toward the ultimate design, I usually discover something that the client absolutely adores: a favorite piece of furniture from a family member, or a painting, a piece of textile, something that I can latch on to.

Most clients can define quite clearly what point in the spectrum from traditional to ultramodern they want to live in, which always suggests the building blocks for the mix of textures. I've never had a client say, "Oh, I don't know whether I want to be eighteenth-century rococo or twenty-first-century futurist or eclectic." Everybody can define that, because the answer doesn't depend on surfaces. It comes from our experiences, and from the air of the times we live in, and from the texture that experience gives to our lives.

Every interior designer continues to discover the history of objects, which, after all, are not only art but also memory made tangible. The texture of life resonates on the surface of things made by hand. I've draped the table in silk damask, a type of weave developed in Renaissance Italy. Atop the table are two nineteenth-century vases and a twentieth-century silver bowl. The semigloss wall paint provides a wonderful background for the contemporary art.

054

Our appreciation of the decorative arts, of the things that man has always created to express and to accoutre the well-lived life, generally deepens and expands over time. It's rare today to find someone who cultivates the arts of the hand, yet there's nothing more glamorous than having some-thing made especially for you — by the person who is the very best in the world at a disappearing art. Elizabeth Dow hand-painted and glazed the wall covering in this foyer, with furniture from Holly Hunt, photographs by Alexandra Penney, and floor tiles of Indian marble from Paris Ceramics.

Elizabeth Dow's matte silver leaf paper shimmers on the walls of this darkly dramatic, almost operatically rich dining room. To create an impression of height, I had the moldings at the ceiling hand-painted with a faux *ivoire* finish: they bring the eye up (yes, I use texture the same way I use all my other favorite design tools: to add motion to a space) to the cloud-painted ceiling.

It's possible to create a thick, yet suave, interior impasto — a rich and varied sense of texture — using highly refined materials and ultraluxe finishes. Here, a deliciously heavy silk satin from Schumacher is pleated and swagged, and detailed with horsehair borders on the jabots and bobbin bead fringe. The black lacquered Biedermeier furniture shines under a nineteenth-century silvered and gilded Austrian chandelier. The table sparkles with crystal goblets on hefty stems sized for the palm, not the fingertips, gold-trimmed porcelain, and ivory-handled cutlery. In the corner, I've set a 1950s screen: it's the city of Chicago, leafed in gold, silver, and copper.

I upholstered the walls of the formal dining room in one of New York's finest remaining early-twentieth-century mansions in the same elegant wool damask that I used on chairs. The faux *marbre* columns connect this room to the foyer. Draperies and chairs are trimmed with handmade passementeries.

One of a designer's many challenges is that of making an entrance, so to speak. When the opportunity arises, and you've got a chance to create a magnificent sense of procession into the heart of the house, take it. This house positively required a grand statement for the foyer. I lavished my attention on the surfaces. The walls are glazed in multiple tones of yellow, and a pumice and mahogany settee sits straight-backed and stern against the wall. A remarkable micro-mosaic table takes pride of place.

This 1860s table illustrates one of the many decorative obsessions of that era: the walnut base features a winged sphinx. The carving is deep and extraordinarily detailed. The table, the center of attention, sports a rare micro-mosaic top. The marble floors were custom designed and made to order in Italy.

Most people think of texture in purely tactile terms, such as rough, smooth, nubbly, and so on. I love the sensuality of surface quality, but I also like to create texture through the visual contrast of matte and shiny, transparent and opaque, etc. Here, both types of texture play hard — but not hard to get. I've done heavy metal, but lightly, and I've gone for the plush: white gold-leaf armchair frames, stainless-steel table bases, woven stainless sheers hanging on matte nickel rods, silver threads in the sofa's velvet, and silk and chenille on the Jean-Michel Frank chairs.

Color, texture, and luster are equal partners when it comes to endowing a room with enduring visual interest and tactile pleasure.

The client's antique silver sits serenely atop this very geometric side table, which rises from an angular base; the interior is rose-colored, yet another variation on the bevy of pinks used in this room. Flecks of Lurex add sparkle to the velvet upholstery.

Throw pillows add to the medley of textures collected in this room. The large leaf pattern on the cut-velvet pillow is pretty in pink, and it relates to the Andy Warhol print and the design of the heavily figured silver bowl. The silk check pillow is trimmed with a thick rope.

The glamour of texture is the invitation to touch. If the curve elicits a come-hither call, surface texture sings a siren's song ...

Details, details, details! It's all in the details. Layer after layer of molding works its way up through this London bedroom, which gives the eye plenty of treats, from the fretwork of the window-seat base to the surround of the bay to the ceiling trim. Hand-painted parchment covers the walls.

Textures can be subtle or shocking and everything in between. Here, I used flat paint on the walls, a raw silk to upholster the bed, quilted-cotton bedcovers, Shantung shadow-striped silk for the curtains, and a hand-hooked wool rug. Natural cowhide on the chair and mercury-glass lamps add even more intrigue.

I call this interior my "sentimental" room, because the design is all about the texture of time — from the tea-stained look of the walls to the button-tufted floral-upholstered slipper chairs. We used a special technique, with a walnut-tinted wax, for the Venetian-plaster-finished wall to create a surface that looks like overlapping panels of leather. Grandma's bedside tables nestle sweetly on either side of a bed that is upholstered and trimmed with nailheads on horsehair. Two of the pillows are encased in vintage gold-bullion-embroidered muslin from Jack Lenor Larsen. Coin dots are always currencies of style.

It comes from our experiences, and from the air of the times we live in, and from the texture that experience gives to our lives.

I wanted the living room of this New York
residence to feel like a classic French salon. Hence the *boiserie*,
which was finished with a multistage process that involved glazing,
stippling, and strié. I used various tonalities of the same color —
radiating from the lightest shade in the center panel to more
saturated color on the perimeter — to give the walls great depth.
The gilded Boulle cabinet features pewter and brass inlays on ebony,
with a marble top.

A chair dressed in cut velvet sits next to a leather-topped
Russian table. Austrian enameled tole sconces bloom delicately at
eye height; a Savonnerie carpet spreads across the parquet.

This library has the **wonderful** color and glow of a bottle of fine cognac when it's held up to the light. The upper walls are finished with a double strié glaze that was finished with steel wool to heighten the texture, which now has the slubbed look of an old Venetian velvet. Marbleized moldings and baseboards, which I added to frame the space, balance the volume and make it cozier. The seventeenth-century Pietra Dura marble tabletop was, in fact, the first piece purchased for the room and inspired the color scheme and the choice of fabrics.

For this extremely elegant powder room

I assembled a collage of textures by layering luxe material atop luxe material and filigreed pattern atop filigreed pattern. The multicolored stone of the basin — the same stone as the floor tiles — has been hand-carved into shallow flutes. A wool-and-silk blend in a saturated shade of elephant gray upholsters the walls. Black-and-gold gimp, tightly woven, helps to frame perimeters outlined by black lacquered moldings and baseboards. Gold-leafed sconces, elaborately shaped and ornamented fittings, and gilded brackets provide a necessary lustrous gleam.

The powder room walls radiate a lavalike heat, thanks to their Etruscan-red sponged finish. The sink bowl, carved from a solid block of red jasper, rests on a fluted column of bronze. The mirror sits in a bronze frame enlivened by a classic egg-and-dart motif. The silk at the window softens the hard surfaces.

Texture is also a measure of age, a level of patina, a degree of refinement.

I often use pattern to create the kind of visual texture that appeals so strongly to me. For example, the custom hinged window panels of this jewel box of a powder room consist of milk glass set in a bronze fretwork that's been laser-cut to reiterate the pattern of the red jasper and white marble mosaic on the floor. The antique French commode sports white marble panels and a white marble top. A series of Rembrandt etchings hangs insouciantly on the wall.

Each temperament of texture exists in endless variation, and the options are limitless.

This room is a twentieth-century French confection that takes its particular chromatic splendor from the glass paperweights that the client collects, each of which blossoms into a miniature cosmos, a kaleidoscopic display of color, light, and pattern. An Art Deco poster hangs on the wall.

The shape of the sofa and the mass of the ottoman, the shagreen-embossed leather upholstery, the leopard print, the use of Schiaparelli's famous "hot pink," the low-slung yet still lithe frame of the side chair all contribute to a sensibility of elegant and luxurious sophistication.

Texture can be far more than just an inducement for the eye to set the hand in motion. At its most evocative, texture creates a very special kind of drama.

077

A custom-made ebonized tray with a strong wood grain and smart silver handles rests atop the oversize ottoman and displays the collection of paperweights. The South American seed pods that stretch alongside add a gutsy, eccentric touch of nature's own textural exploits — adding yet another variable to the algebra of visual complexity.

Color.

I n the height of the fall foliage season, when I'm driving down the expressway, I always dream that I will actually figure out how to create a room that has that same magical dappling of light, shape, and color.

Translating a single tint, much less an entire palette, from nature poses the ultimate challenge for anyone who works with color. How, for example, can you possibly find a literal, tactile, tangible translation of a particular moment — that instant, that one hue, that you'd like to freeze from the constantly changing incandescent luminosity that is a sunset? Honestly, I think it's only possible, really, with new technology — and with light — because there's so much there that's not about surface. It's about air and the atmosphere, and how can you capture that?

Everything that I do begins with color. As a child I liked my fort and my junkyard, but I was absolutely besotted with anything related to color: my rainbow of pencils, my crayons, my pastels, my watercolor set, my acrylics — all those wonderful ranges and densities and qualities of color. Of course I had the biggest set of each, and I used them constantly and ravenously. Nothing excited me more than playing with color: I experimented with mixing and layering shades and mediums, with creating new tints and tones. I thrived on the possibilities and on discovering what might happen when I applied different degrees of pressure, what intensity of feeling I

could summon from those colors — from the ethereal to the riotous profusion to the well-placed wallop.

My first fascination with color's mysteries and emotive powers has never dulled. I know that my interest in what I saw at my father's printing company has only increased over time and that my delight in the marvelously mushy, shiny, thick, viscous inks that I coveted at his factory has never waned. Nor has my pleasure in the tools of color diminished. I still remember how the pressmen slathered those inks onto rollers with spatulas and the utterly precise wizardry they executed with industrial technology.

Thanks to Parsons, I learned the immutable rules of classic color theory: shades and tints, hues and tones, the color wheel, complementary and primary colors. The course emphasized that color exists only in the presence of light and that changing light alters your perception and appreciation of color — of course the nature of light also transforms the nature of color. Think about how useful that information is to the designer and what it allows you to do for your client: after all, there are no mystery paints (particularly when you take pigment straight from a can). But it is possible to seduce even an eye that knows otherwise into the belief that four walls painted the same color are actually four walls limned in different colors.

All designers develop their own devices for manipulating color in space. One of my favorites is to use a single color in a range of textural and tonal mutations throughout a room so that it appears as a chromatic scale from pastel hues to full saturation, each note of which is affected by any lustrous elements in the room. Suppose that you take the same exact shade of a particular yellow, for example, and repeat it in various materials — some that absorb light, others that reflect light — each yellow, although it's exactly the same shade as the others, will appear to differ from the others simply because of the interaction between the material and light.

There are many ways to derive a palette. Natural materials, for example, naturally have color. Woods provide an innate multihued palette, from the cooler browns of walnut to the reddish browns of cherry to the blonds of maple and ash to the warmer browns of mahogany, which often veer toward purple or magenta or plum. You can create wonderful, colorful effects by applying aniline stains to wood. They emphasize the pattern of the grain but in Technicolor, so to speak: lavender oak, for example, or magenta bird's-eye maple. Marbles and stones come in myriad shades and hues as well. Even if you're looking at a natural neutral, such as beige limestone, different quarries yield stones of many different colors: that beige limestone can appear gray or warm beige or pink or mauve naturally.

Among my favorite hues are the strong, saturated, highly spicy shades common to the hot climates — the African and Asian countries, North Africa and Morocco, and, of course, India — because they definitely pack a punch. Each culture has its individual color customs, its own way with the pinks and the reds and the oranges, all mixed together in incredible intensities.

I love all colors of the rainbow. Even those that I thought were not my favorites I've come to adore. Twenty years ago, I wouldn't have hesitated to banish yellow and blue from my palette. In fact, I did. Oddly enough, they have probably been America's two favorites for generations, and now I embrace them wholeheartedly. For the last four years, my own bedroom has been an ode to yellow — actually, to a saturated sunshine shade of chrome yellow that's not unlike the brilliantly translucent saffron of nineteenth-century Peking glass. I have never thought of myself as a yellow person — perhaps that was part of my personal rebellion against the princes and princesses of chintz, and against the self-consciously well-mannered understatement of, say, the kind of butter-yellow drawing room that the famed English decorator Nancy Lancaster installed.

All sorts of things pique my color sense and inspire my color palette, from the panoply of shades that is a leaf over the course of its life to the flowers in a summer garden, from the 120 screens in a Chuck Close print to the Gene Davis silkscreens that I loved as a child. One of my favorite things is an amazing English candlestick that I found in a Bleecker Street antiques shop: it's a massive, late-nineteenth-century piece made of glass, with a glass spiral coiled around the shaft, the entire thing a shade of purple so deep that it reads as black. You could not find a piece that looks more modern, yet it's not. You could not find something that looks more like black, but, of course, it's not. It embodies everything that color is for me: my personal Rosebud.

When I approach a project, color is the element I naturally go to first. My inspiration can come from an object or an impression, or from something in nature. Sometimes I select colors because of a specific chromatic idea that I want to explore. While I tend to prefer solids, occasionally I go for the gusto of a gutsy pattern — as in the case of this powder room. The palette is my personal response to the Gene Davis prints, which hang nearby. I devised the grid and played with the placement of each hue. Each four-inch square is individually painted, and the effect is kaleidoscopic.

Because my mother loved art, we went to museum after museum after museum: the Wadsworth Athenaeum in Hartford, all of New York's wonderful museums and galleries, and other cultural hot spots in the region. That early exposure influences me to this day. I've always loved art that, like this series of Gene Davis prints, is lively and colorful, with a lot of movement. The 1,001 colors in these prints established the palette for this room: fuchsia walls and a fuchsia lacquered table top, with blue and purple accents. Pattern comes from the art, the flocking on the iridescent silk curtains, and the tie-dyed patent-leather upholstery.

Every designer develops his or her own color sense and sensibility, and it changes over time. I never thought I'd have yellow fever, but here we are. This bedroom is an ode to a saturated shade of sunshine. Black accents and zebra stripes anchor the interior.

I've used the same chrome yellow in varying textures and tonalities throughout — at the windows, on the walls, for upholstery, and as accents on the bed. In fact, the whole apartment is a play on applying color in different textures and tonalities: one predominant color per room, one accent to punch things up or settle things down, and details (like the black welting on the chairs) that punctuate the larger color statement.

I love all colors of the rainbow. Even those that were not my favorites I've come to adore.

The visitors to Gracie Mansion often enter
through the foyer of the Wagner wing, added in the 1960s. I had
the walls painted a warm sand tone, a simple neutral made more
interesting by marbleizing it in big blocks. The extraordinarily
vibrant blue of the stair runner establishes a sense of ceremony
and leads the eye directly to the ballroom beyond. Because that
fabulous fifty-by-twenty-four-foot space would be used for
innumerable press conferences, I wanted it to be telegenic and
photogenic as well as stately and ceremonial, hence the magnificent Wedgwood blue of the Venetian plaster walls.

White moldings set off the deep,
double-glazed cobalt walls of the second drawing
room, which is adjacent to the ballroom. The blue
offsets the rich red tones of the mahogany.

Each culture has its individual color customs, its own way with the pinks and the reds and the oranges, all mixed together in incredible intensities.

Gracie Mansion's library adjoins the dining room, so I had the rug woven with medallions in the exact same shades of green and gold. The vibrant turquoise, a French blue, was popular with Americans in the mid-nineteenth century — it comes straight from the dining room's Zuber paper. The wallpaper border brings the gold on the floor up to the ceiling; I've continued the color onto the ceiling and into the ovolo framework. Custom-woven silk damask drapes the windows.

Gracie Mansion once served as the first home of the Museum of the City of New York, and it's been the mayor's official residence since the administration of Fiorello H. La Guardia. The renovation was a challenging task because significant work needed to be done on the house before the decorating could begin. We got to the fun part, however, in short order. I was thrilled to discover that the Federalists' color sense was so similar to my own. Many of the antiques have long been in the collection of the Gracie Mansion Conservancy, including the magnificent sideboard once owned by the Gracies. I added the circa-1810 French chandelier to complement the Zuber paper.

In Gracie Mansion's formal dining room, opposite the parlor, I've taken the yellow and green story in a new direction. Eminent designer Albert Hadley installed the period scenic wallpaper — Zuber's *Les Jardins de France* — in the 1984 renovation; the scenic paper helps smooth the distinctive chromatic transition between the two rooms. One of Manhattan's oldest surviving wood structures, it dates to 1799. Built by Archibald Gracie, a Scottish-born merchant, the house once welcomed such revolutionary leaders as the Marquis de Lafayette, John Quincy Adams, and George Washington.

Many people are shocked when they learn that our forebears loved saturated color and used it liberally, and even, sometimes, with abandon. For the recent renovation of Gracie Mansion, the official residence of the mayor of New York City, I did extensive research, as one must when working on a historic restoration. This saturated shade of yellow dates to the early nineteenth-century Federal era, when it was called Patent Yellow. A medley of greens grounds that explosion of color, and the gilded accents add a touch of levity. Although it is furnished in period style, I've arranged the parlor for modern use.

There are many ways to derive a palette. Natural materials, for example, naturally have color.

Gracie Mansion's private quarters are also period style. The color story in the State Bedroom — a medley of mauves, creams, chocolate, and rose — dates to the later Victorian era, in comparison to the rest of the décor from the early nineteenth century. The bamboo furniture, which the Conservancy acquired, is circa 1880.

Natural light floods the Susan B. Wagner drawing room, so I used a color palette that was rather more delicate than elsewhere, one that would blossom in the sun. Shades of apricot provide the basis for my favorite tone-on-tone treatment. I always use color to draw the eye around the room, sometimes in surprisingly subtle ways. Here the ceiling is limned in a pale blue. Yes, it beckons the eye upward — and it quietly ignites a glow in the various shades of apricot below.

The State Sitting Room is definitely exotic, but the green wainscoting tones down the fabulous floral wallpaper. The rug's field is the same shade; the border picks up the oranges in the wallpaper. The lounge chairs and sofas take the same tone, with a variant used in the detail on the side chairs.

I like to throw in off-notes of color to give the room more complexity and to give it punch, and I think that approach is absolutely reasonable even in a historic interior. Here shots of orange and yellow on pillows and lamp bases enliven what is, apart from the wallpaper, essentially a single-color scheme.

My first fascination with color's mysteries and emotive powers has never dulled.

In this room, as I often do, I played a game of theme and variations. Obviously, the dominant shade of blue limns the walls. But I also used several other closely related hues: the blue felt on the pool table comes from the same turquoise family, as do the dyed cowhides that border the room. The bench is upholstered in yet another relative of the primary shade, this time darker. The Calder mobile helps to animate the air space overhead. There's something particularly fun about these little glass tables: they add some reflective notes, teasing the eye without blocking the view.

This is an enormous room, with seventeen-foot-high ceilings, so I enveloped it in color to make it as intimate as possible. Why blue? It's true that billiard rooms tend to be wood paneled, well oiled, and fitted out with lots of brass accoutrements — and of course the billiard balls add spots of color, but this one takes pride of place in a vast residence on the eighty-ninth floor of a Manhattan skyscraper; the view through that wall of windows is astonishing. This glorious shade of blue matches the sky at precisely that moment before the horizon goes dark and the world is washed in indigo.

This sitting room is my little serenade to serendipity, to my beloved Kenneth Noland striped prints, and to Chuck Close, among my favorite modern artists, whose self-portrait hangs above the sofa. The exuberant shades of kumquat leap directly from Noland's prints onto the walls and into the room, as do the contrasting colors.

I really wanted this room to vibrate with color. You can see very clearly the devices that I use to spread color around the room, and the complex effect that occurs when you play with one color in a range of finishes and materials — shimmering upholstered walls, shatteringly saturated velvet upholstery, sunshiny high-gloss lacquer.

Translating a single tint, much less an entire palette, from nature poses the ultimate challenge for anyone who works with color.

Among my favorite hues are the strong, saturated, highly spicy shades common to the hot climates . . . because they definitely pack a punch.

If you want beige, don't come to me. I like surprises, and I work very hard to make sure that each room I design has plenty of them. In other words, I don't want people to be satisfied with just one look. I've gone through phases with color: I've had my orchid period, my blue period, my yellow period. This room is from my tangerine period. The rug is one of my designs for Roubini.

I love mixing high design with everyday objects, wonderful antiques, and flea market finds. This ceiling fixture, for example, is a 1950s treasure. Its whimsical form and sassy, candy-colored glass diffusers suited me — and the room and the client — just perfectly.

I always try to find color palettes that match the client's personality, and sometimes it's like pulling teeth. Most people, even if they love color, are afraid to live with it. But in this case, there were plenty of clues to suggest possible palettes. As you can see from her wardrobe, this client *ain't* afraid of color. In fact, she loves color just as much as I do, which made for an exceptionally gratifying process.

While I did apply broad strokes of color to this apartment, if you look carefully, you'll see that there's lots of white space, literally and metaphorically. In the client's boudoir, I used intense color on the floor and the furnishings. There's a rainbow array of pillows, and lavender walls, but the frame for the interior is neutral: white storage space, white moldings, and so on.

The room for which I was dubbed "the King of Color" happens, basically, to be neutral. The palette consists of chrome yellow, bittersweet chocolate brown, and Bristol blue, deployed strategically. The large central ottoman provides the biggest jolt of color: the saturated shade of the vintage linen velvet upholstery, plus the matching chaise pillows, the seventeen-foot-high curtains, and the glass and Minton accessories definitely make this room sing — but not the blues.

Simple palettes that are easily read have great strength and, quite often, great allure.

Chrome yellow may not be the subtlest of shades, but it is always radiant and well suited to an enormous, sun-drenched country house room. It also lightens and brightens the blues. The 1840s Baltic mahogany and gilt armchairs have been covered in yellow-dyed cowhide and accented with nailhead trim.

The dahlia-strewn 1960s rug gave seed to the parchment wall treatment in this Hamptons library. Seven related shades of red — a full spectrum, from the deepest Chinese coral, or cinnabar, to the ripest cantaloupe — heat up a book-lined interior that features a Jansen table and lots of comfortable seating. The paintings against the wall are mine: I was inspired by the light reflecting off a new skyscraper in New Haven, and I did them when I was fifteen. The white bouclé on the wing chair relates to the room's white-painted woodwork: it is both punctuation and visual relief.

I'm still as fascinated by color as I was as a child, and I continue to surprise myself with my ever-changing tastes in tonal palettes. Pink? Yes. Aqua? Yes. Orange? No surprise. I'm sure that my youthful visits to my father's printing company planted the seeds of my particular way of seeing color, and of seeing that the impossible, in terms of color, didn't really exist. I'm also sure that those visits fostered both my love of the shiny and my delight in the printed image — such as the parrot tulips here, which provided the impetus for the palette of this room.

Think pink? I think so. The hot pink of the draped walls reflects off the mirrored and etched surfaces of the desk. In fact, the mirror cools the overheated space down. The oak parquet floor is stained two shades of pink. The zebra stripes bring the pattern up from the floor.

Use a single color in a range of textural and tonal mutations throughout a room so that it appears as a chromatic scale from pastel hues to full saturation ...

I like to have some point of departure when I begin thinking about a color palette for a project. It may be something that the client has — a rug that they love, perhaps, or a piece of art that we can build a scheme around. The departure point may also be just their preferences and the nature of the room: Should it be warm and intimate, or a jewel box, or more fresh and airy? Is it a weekend house or a city house? What's the climate? All these issues affect our decisions about the color palettes we'll use.

Clients usually get a little shy about talking about the colors they like, but you can usually elicit that by talking about what colors you don't like. "Let's rule out what doesn't feel good to you," I'll say. Or, "Do you prefer brighter tones? Do you prefer inkier tones? Do you like jewel tones? Do you like brighter pastels?" From there we sashay forth.

There's nothing like the intensity of color, the saturated depth of color that you can get from a fantastic linen or cotton or mohair velvet. That's why I love using different types of fabrics in the same color family. I think color should make the eye move throughout the room: colored lampshades may anchor the room's corners, and throw pillows can help spread that color through the space. The secondary color adds a pleasurable little jolt. It may show up as a wash of color on the ceiling to move the eye upward, but it always creates another level of complexity and definition.

This bedroom is something of a sonata in shades of orchid, with my signature repetition of a particular hue in a variety of textures. But even I know not to overdo things. That's why the chairs are upholstered in a neutral color, and why the bedspread, bolster, and lampshades are off-white.

All sorts of things
pique my color
sense and inspire my
color palette, from
the panoply of
shades that is a leaf
over the course of its
life to the flowers in
a summer garden.

My point of departure for a color palette often comes from something I find in nature, and here's a perfect example of that. Clearly, the petals of these gorgeous anemones suggested the rest of the palette. In fact, the hand-colored shagreen on the tabletop is a perfect foil.

The Curve.

A sense of geometry and a feeling for elemental forms are two of any designer's not-so-secret weapons when it comes to creating a harmonious interior.

I'm calling this chapter "The Curve," but I could just as easily have called it "The Square" or "The Triangle" or "The Octagon" or "The Hexagon." For me, though, a curve has a kind of natural appeal. It is an embrace — and an easement. It welcomes you, and it allows you freedom of **motion**.

We all tend to concentrate on the profile, that line of many possibilities that we see in two dimensions. It's important to understand what period and what culture each piece comes from, and the profile generally provides us with the best visual shorthand of a piece's stylistic heritage, which is useful when we begin to devise a plan for a room. Although we sometimes have the luxury of working on projects where the clients are starting afresh, from scratch, more often than not we're working with clients who have possessions that they've either inherited or collected. We also frequently confront projects where the clients have had the good fortune to travel extensively and who, like most of us, have brought something home from each stop that they've made around the world. It's my job to figure out the common threads and how we can and should put these things — and additional ones — together. Very often, it's the profile that leads the way.

I don't generally take a strict academic approach to most of my projects. In other words, form is not so formulaic for me. I'm not particularly interested in the kind of historical verisimilitude that, say, drives those designers who develop restoration dramas for today's décor. I think that living in a historical shadowbox at home is inappropriate for most of us, if not a little stultifying, and rather uncomfortable for our guests. I do recognize, however, that when someone chooses to inhabit that kind of environment, it's a choice that emerges from a deep passion and a singularly focused intellect. How can you not admire that?

There are cases, though, where recreating the interior design of a bygone era down to the last detail is utterly appropriate. Gracie Mansion, which I had the honor to restore, was that kind of project for me: it has historic importance architecturally and is also a showpiece for both New York City and America. One handles such a project with great care, and only after much research.

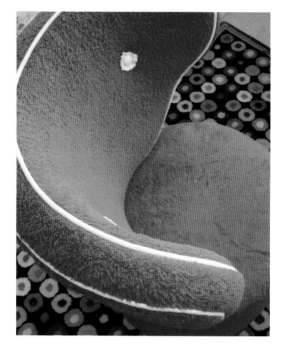

One of the ways that I bring cohesion to my projects is by choreographing the repetition of form in space: horizontally, vertically, orthogonally, and at an angle, at all different **levels** and planes within the volume of the room. Finding a motif and then reiterating it on various scales helps me not only to select each component of the décor, but also to weave them into an intricate, coherent fabric that has visible strength and resonance. What I do with **form** is in many respects similar to the way I treat color, but I think it's much more subtle because it often takes a while for the eye to realize what's going on in front of it, behind it, and overhead. Most people respond to color first, with an immediate and emotional reaction. I like color to pack a wallop, to engage and delight the eye, to lift the spirits, to bring the space to life. But when it comes to the **repetition** of form, I want my clients and their visitors to discover things over time — as a lovely series of little surprises. I

the dramatic swoosh of the leg, the strong **arch** of the seat front or chair back. That kind of bold design gesture delights me. Fortunately, such gestures recur at almost regular intervals in the history of the decorative arts. You'll find them in, among other things, Art Deco chairs from the 1920s, in Biedermeier chairs from the 1840s, in the re-creations of Louis XVI chairs that the great House of Jansen did in the 1940s, and in the many contemporary chairs by designers such as John Boone,

don't think that when most people walk into one of my rooms, they say, "Oh, look, he's used circles again and again and again."

The repetition of form can either oppose or embrace the surrounding architecture, and the choice is different for each project. I'm currently working on a 1960s house that has a hexagonal living room, with all sorts of bizarre star-pointed rooms that shoot off from it. In this project, you can't escape the **hexagon**, so we've decided to emphasize it as much as possible. We've chosen some wonderful Frank Lloyd Wright hexagonal tables and a sofa angled at the precise 37-degree angle as the wall behind it — and that's just the beginning. In other rooms, in other houses, you'll sometimes find that you prefer the tension created by a contrast of forms, whether you square the **circle** or circle the square — installing beaded circular molding, for example, in a severe rectangular room.

I love circles and curves in all their endless variations. You'll very often find a range of armchairs in my projects, each with its own distinct case of the bends: the sweeping curl of the arm, the loose or tight **spiral** of the elbow,

whose furniture from the 1990s is so happily voluptuous. And yet, these extremely diverse designs cohabit together peacefully, thanks to their complementary curves.

Throughout each room of each project, I tend to explore the curve or square or whatever form is dominant, almost ad infinitum. A circular dining table, a round ottoman, the drops of a chandelier, the **conical** lampshades, the rounded corners of a Turkish-cornered pillow — these are all things that use the similar vocabulary of the curve in ways that create very comfortable and cohesive spaces and a terrific sense of movement. Circular tables seem to provide more options for me than square pieces, for example, when it comes to arranging the other furniture. Round things and curved things seem to me to take up less air space, which is why I think I have a special fondness for circular end tables and lamp tables. Not only is creating a **path** around them easier, but they also seem, at least to me, to make the room dance. Is there anything more glamorous than that?

There's no denying geometry, especially in places where the human body is vulnerable and exposed. Sharply angled edges can easily injure, so I often soften them with a bullnose and smooth out the hard corners. Curves sweep through several different planes in the volume of this bath and contrast with straight lines and hard angles. You can't escape a curve in the bath: the entire space is about touch. The slope and lip of the basins reflect the slope and lip of the tub, while the snaking profile of the vanity counter built for two curls snugly around the waist.

Every designer has a kind of tool chest filled with the favorite devices that he or she uses to bring harmony to a space. My personal preference depends on a sense of basic geometry and form. Because I like rooms to have a sense of movement — to dance, really — I tend to try to choreograph form, to use the repetition of form and line throughout a space to energize it. When you do that, it's critical that you remember to think of whatever form or shape it is in three dimensions. In a bathroom, curves are essential to comfort — and so inescapable.

Here's how I square the circle: a large central ottoman, Turkish corners on the pillows, chair arms from different centuries with complementary curves (the 1930s Austrian Art Deco chairs are by Christian Krass, the gilded French chair dates from the 1840s), and, of course, the painting.

Form is amplitude as well as outline. I like height, and I find it extremely glamorous. I always mount the curtains at the highest possible point on a wall, and I always incorporate any space above the window into that elevation. Rooms should stand tall and proud: if you mount the curtains directly over the window frame, with three more feet of wall rising, unadorned, to the ceiling, you have a room that slouches.

I love circles and curves in all their endless variations.

This loft apartment has a relatively open plan, with the dining room adjacent to the living room. The round dining table with its patinated steel finish provides an antidote to the orthogonal wall arrangement that frames the space. The Schiaparelli sofa that marks the boundary of the living room is a Michael Taylor classic.

The repetition of form can either oppose or embrace the surrounding architecture.

You can see how cuckoo I was for curves here, from the scalloped edges of the bookshelf to the voluptuously easy line of the chair profile and back, to the melting edges of Salvador Dalí's softly curvaceous clock face, to the ringed candlestick.

Throughout each room of each project, I tend to explore the curve or square or whatever form is dominant, almost ad infinitum.

I find that I very often use circular tables — as well as ovals and racetrack shapes for dining, coffee, and occasional pieces — because I think the absence of corners helps create the perception that the room is larger than it may in fact be. Certainly it's a whole lot easier to move around a curved surface. The seating is plump and designed for maximum comfort, from graciously curved backs to gently curved legs to generously rolled arms.

This operatic space is filled with voluptuous, oversize curves, which suits its occupant, a world-renowned opera manager, to a do-re-mi. The round center table is Swedish and dates from the 1930s. We accessorized with pieces of Venetian glass (the client's heritage is Italian), gilded metal sconces, and acid-green mercury-glass lamps.

The curlicues of the loop-de-looping arms of the chandelier over the dining room table echo the sinuously curved petals of the giant gilded fleur-de-lis set prominently along the mirrored wall. The chair backs bend out gracefully into the space around the circular table.

This is my "candle in the wind" room, a style statement that seems utterly appropriate to a contemporary urban loft. Minimalism is in, as we all know. Something about the heavy editing of contemporary spaces makes the details much more visible — and much more immediate — than they appear in other, more decorated, rooms. You might call the textures in this space subtle, or virtually nonexistent. After all, the only things that break the perfect surfaces are the nailhead trim and the softly sueded face of the chair upholstery.

One of the ways I bring cohesion to my projects is by choreographing the repetition of form in space . . .

How well do I love the curve? Let me count the ways that form is repeated here. There are the interlocking curlicues of the painting, the attenuated, softened H of the chair frame, the roll of the sofa arm, the cushy corners of the throw cushions, and the lovely ceramic bowls on the table — and that's just the beginning.

There is nothing quite like Euclidean geometry: form and pattern cannot — do not — exist independently of point, line, and plane. Sometimes it's fun to really emphasize the relationship that a line has to a point, and to a plane, and to a surface. In this room, the light-hearted loop-de-loops of the wrought-iron chandelier add a cheery, and I think witty, gloss on the astonishing cornucopia of curves, arcs, circles, and spheres that provide the ornamental motifs for not only the table setting but the overall décor of the room.

Possibilities abound for inventive ways to make visual statements through repetition. A wall of framed images — all of the same dimension, each with a different subject or illustration — can definitely make you sit up and take notice. Here, the photographic series of a major installation by the glass artist Dale Chihuly completely animates the wall. The rigor of the framing and placement organizes the riot of color and form. Léger's and Chihuly's palettes range widely over similar parts of the spectrum. In a room such as this, the eye delights because there is always, always, always something new to discover.

Every design has a kind of genetic code, even if you're not always aware of the characteristics of the original design DNA as you make your selections and work out the details. This room, however, quite obviously owes its existence to that fabulous Léger tapestry on the wall. The soft forms of the seating, the plump curves of the pillows, the gentle rise of the ottoman, and the arms of the chair, which slope like the shoulders and arms of the figures — all derive from the tapestry's forms. The color palette, too, comes straight off the wall.

Finding a motif and then reiterating it on various scales helps me not only to select each component of the décor, but also to weave them into an intricate, coherent fabric that has visible strength and resonance.

The curve rules — the chandelier and candelabras, the table, the rug, the lovely lines of the porcelain vases. The clean, crisp lines of the sideboard and the startling statement of its orange ponyskin doors prevent the room from spinning into utter loopiness. I picked the rug's colors from the porcelains.

Fashion is an endless font of inspiration for those delicious details that finish a room.

Circular tables seem
to provide more
options for me than
square pieces when
it comes to arranging
the other furniture.

I am fascinated by
jewelry, and I have a particular
passion for cabochon-cut stones in
sleek, gold settings, a passion that
inspired this rug that I designed for
Roubini. I find the symmetry between
the concentric patterns of the onyx
tabletop and the ensorcelled circles on
the floor quite delightful.

The
Mix.

The power to transform is utterly, completely glamorous — at least to me. I've always enjoyed being a bit of a chameleon, especially when it comes to matters of decorating styles. Frankly, I think I'd be very bored if I did the same thing day in and day out, over and over again, although I admire those designers who do, and do it well. Much of my own unending joy in interior design, however, comes from the challenge of deciphering who my clients are and using my particular strengths and talents to fashion the **collage**: the olio of objects that reflects their personalities.

Putting things together is one of the trickiest parts of what any designer does. Editorial skills matter. The practiced ability to consider objects, colors, forms, and textures with a critical, educated, and truly disciplined eye requires nerve and decisiveness as well as training. You have to know, *really know*, what works and what doesn't, both for your client and for yourself. That assertion of sense and sensibility is probably the most **intuitive** aspect of design, not only for me but also for the client: it's the client, after all, who must make that leap of faith when it comes to my suggestions for the exuberant choices, for **juxtapositions** that may not seem right, much less fabulous, until they exist in three-dimensional reality in a room.

The mix almost always begins at home, just like everything else. I

probably made my first stabs at the recombinative art in my childhood fort, cobbling together a décor out of bottles and wash pans, washboards, basins, old farm implements, and tractor seats. While the stuff definitely came from the present (however much I thought of my junk treasures as antiques), each piece was probably made of a material different from the others. I'm sure it was the variety of patinas — from dirt to rust — that appealed to my eye, and that I used to make our space a happening one.

Later, in the 1960s, as I was growing up and voraciously devouring shelter magazines, **eclecticism** reached its height. The decorators of that era who were icons for me, and who are probably ripe for rediscovery today, showed all of us how to be free to put things together. Notable among them are Henri Samuel, Ruben de Saavedra, Valerian Rybar, my late cousin Yale Burge, and Angelo Donghia (certainly a little bit later), all of whom produced, practically prestidigitated, superb mixes. Sometimes they applied stringent clarity, and other times they approached things with vast abandon. Albert Hadley, of course, has always been a master of the mix, and I count him as one of my great influences. I can still remember seeing the photographs of the living room he did for the Paleys at the St. Regis: stunning yellow lacquered walls, Boulle furniture, Regence mirror. For me it signified the ultimate evocation of minimal **rich**.

The mix comes from within, from the assuredness that, really, there are no rules. Yes, you can mix styles and periods and cultures. You can indeed hang English Regency chandeliers above a vast mahogany table surrounded by French chairs in a room dominated by a portrait of an American giant — Benjamin Franklin — staring at himself in a vast English Gothic mirror, on the opposite wall, that hovers above Chinese Tang funerary warriors flanked by a pair of Russian vases. To pull that type of mighty **mélange** together requires rigor and confidence, plus a formula for form, scale, and color. But think about it: in one room that lives today, you've just achieved harmony among many cultures and seven hundred years of history.

When a client presents you with seven completely crazy objects that don't relate to each other in any obvious way, it's an incredibly stimulating task to formulate the unifying thread that will bring them all together. That's the kind of **complexity** that keeps me interested in my work. Whatever American city we live in, we all inhabit a space filled with influences from our travels, the things we've acquired, and the experiences that have helped us grow. Rooms can embody that personal history, especially when the design actually reflects the client. Working as a residential interior designer is a very intimate process: the more involved the conversation with the client, the more you can create a space that reflects the client's **definitive** self. Sometimes you ask questions and get truly accurate answers. Sometimes you observe and make educated guesses. The longer the relationship is, the more satisfying it becomes because the vocabulary becomes shorthand, and you know immedi-ately what each client will respond to — and, more important, what is right for him or her.

I prefer to do each room a little more slowly than others might. Ideas don't always jell immediately, and decisions often improve with mulling. Whenever it's possible, I like to say to my clients: "You know what? Why don't we wait and see if we need an extra table over here, or another lamp over there." You can learn a great deal from letting the room evolve a little bit. As the elements **converge** and combine, you begin to have an inkling of what flavor the room will acquire as it settles over time. Nothing is really fixed forever. I change things in my own house, and I'll frequently move things around and add and subtract. If you have a forgiving point of view, you can mix in something new that you're enamored of and move a longtime love a little bit into the shadow.

Diversity is inherently both American and exotic. So, too, is the extraordinary access that we have to information — and to the rest of the world, thanks to twenty-first-century technologies. We have the unprece-dented luxury of limitless opportunity: we can open ourselves to influences from around the world and absorb not only the objects but also the ideas of cultures from different times and places and transform them into something that reflects each of our many different modern lifestyles. There are just two prerequisites: curiosity and energy. Without them, you have nothing. But should you be endowed with both, you can bring all sorts of sundry things together and make peace among them. What could be more glamorous?

An American in London? Yes, and a citizen of the world. For the across-the-pond residence of a New York–based businessman, we reveled in the possibilities for eclecticism. A massive chandelier, still wearing its original, medallion-bedecked glass hurricanes (a theme I borrowed for the custom-designed bronze railings), lights the stairwell. I salvaged the Chinese lacquer panels from a decrepit screen for the long bar cabinet. French sconces flank a painting by Hans Hoffman. A massive eagle-supported English console, flanked by two Chinese Famille Rose cachepots, presides over the landing. Artwise, Warhol's *Nine Marilyns* hangs over a curvaceous Henry Moore. As for the floor, it's antique parquet de Versailles.

The power to transform is utterly, completely glamorous — at least to me.

A collection of civilization's contents suits a grand tourist abroad, in the mode of Mr. Jefferson or Mr. Franklin. The seventeenth-century Roman mantel, supporting a pair of Russian urns, anchors a wall graced by a Regence mirror and a flanking pair of Regence side tables. The Frederick Remington bronze adds a touch of Americana, and manifest destiny. The other art is equally eclectic: a Calder sculpture dances between a pair of French candlesticks underneath a painting by David Smith.

A snappy shock of the new lends piquancy, and glamour, to this intercontinental mix. Jasper Johns's 1961 "0 through 9" series jolts awake a room that, with just its gilded suite of regal French furniture and delirious Neapolitan chandelier, might otherwise have been somewhat on the somnolent side.

Is there anything more flattering, or romantic, than candlelight? I think not, since candles can render glamorous even the most everyday activity. In this room, dinner is served only by candlelight, thanks to four corner torchères, which, with their candelabras, radiate an ambient glow, and a chandelier that takes tapers rather than bulbs. A phalanx of Chinese funerary horses stands in cavalry formation on the sideboard, which also supports a pair of Russian pots.

The juxtaposition of twentieth-century art with eighteenth- and nineteenth-century furniture and objets d'art creates an interesting contrast with the color palette. In the dining room, a Greuze portrait of Benjamin Franklin, painted from life in 1777, hangs over the Irish marble chimneypiece in this London dining room. Two English chandeliers, circa 1820, were originally colza oil lamps; the bronze candelabras in the room's corners are attributed to Francis Remond. The neo-Egyptian silver-gilt epergnes are by Philip Cornman. In the adjacent hall, the silk-screened printer's proof of Jasper Johns's *Flag 1 1973* hangs over a French Empire clock by Dubuc that depicts George Washington.

This room is a careful mix of periods and palette, a luxuriously neutral space brought to life with shots of color. A monumental mixed-media work by Judy Pfaff hangs in its artist-designed frame, enlivening the wall opposite the pillow-strewn upholstered bed. The lamps are twentieth-century designs made of Venetian glass.

Reading in bed is one of life's greater pleasures and minor indulgences, one much beloved by this client — so I've fitted out the bedroom to satisfy her. The bedside tables provide ample storage for favorite books. Lamps with shades that match the curtains cast a sufficiently soft and glare-free glow.

The swooning elegance of the traditional drapery forms come, in this case, from modern materials technology: a next-generation double-faced fabric. A 1940s bench sits at the foot of the bed, and a nineteenth-century chair sits beside it. Nestled on either side of the headboard are late-nineteenth-century black-lacquered Swedish bedside tables.

Diversity is inherently both American and exotic. . . .
There are just two prerequisites: curiosity and energy.

I created this wildly theatrical, heavily ornamented, dizzily operatic scene for my client in the opera business using a mix of patterns carefully selected for their jazziness and seemingly improbable, and improvisational, coherence. The pair of 1950s lamps atop the warm gray bureau feature violin bases. The wall is covered with framed turn-of-the-century and early-twentieth-century hand-colored portraits of opera singers.

The composition of fabric patterns includes a bold purple-and-gray stripe, a large-scale multicolored plaid for the panels of curtains that hang from substantial poles (with a mix of gilt and painted finishes for the rod, finials, and rings), animal prints — of course — and a Chinese scenic for the bed and window shade à la Madama Butterfly. Strategically placed lamps cast dramatic pools of light.

The mirrored wall behind the bed opens up the space visually and reflects the mélange of patterns. The stripes draw the eye up to the pale gray-painted crown molding, which separates the riot of color and pattern below from the creamy, dreamy plane of the pale amber ceiling overhead.

Even a well-trained eye well schooled in the history of the decorative arts can be surprised at times. Care to hazard a date for the fireplace surround? Do you think it "modern"? It was, in the seventeenth century.

In this room, the rules of the game matter. To impose discipline on the decorative, I used the same embroidery in a variety of different ways: on the sofa base, on the pillows, on the window shade.

Snooker, anyone? There cannot be much that is more glamorous than this contemporary billiard room filled with fine antiques and dominated by a Dutch old master. The decidedly ornate nineteenth-century furniture is a matched set; the pieces were made in Britain for the Russian market. The billiard set and its accoutrements are, of course, English; they rest on a magnificent Persian carpet. A bronze fillet frame sets off the grand Dutch old master that takes pride of place on the wall. The contemporary clubby tone of the room emanates from the leather-wrapped panels that upholster the walls.

Some ingredients of this mix are obvious, and obviously me: the high-contrast complements of delphinium and tangerine, the strategic use of black and white accents to provide visual muscle, the introduction of an animal print, and the subdued but richly ornamental carpet on the floor.

There's a high-low component, however, that may not be immediately apparent. On the table, above, each vessel displays the kind of pure formal beauty that has appealed to the eye from the beginning of time: the twentieth-century glass bowl is Swedish, the tall vase is Japanese, and the smaller one is a $3 find.

There are as many ways to develop the right mix for any given job as there are menus to assemble, recipes to follow, and revelries to enjoy. In this case, the client wanted something that would be both casual and formal. A dilemma? A contradiction? Perhaps, perhaps not. The solution here involved a selection of comfy and cushy lounge seating — the sofa and chairs — with more formal, lustrous accents. A little glitter can go a long way toward bringing glamour to a cozy combination. Just look at the reflected glory that the gilded table confers on the velvet-covered Edwardian club chairs.

I call this room the Tangerine Twist, because the success of the entire mix depends on the consistent use of the dominant color — my beloved tangerine. Yes, I've shaded the walls in tones of tangerine and apricot, and upholstered the side chairs and the occasional throw pillow also. The drapes and valances add still more layers of lusciousness to the happily taut visual drama with shadings of orange and terra-cotta. I've carried the use of color as theme down to the smallest, most incidental elements in the room: the basket of tangerines and the candles on the coffee table.

If you have a forgiving point of view, you can mix in something new that you're enamored of and move a longtime love a little bit into the shadow.

Every once in an orange moon, a designer happens onto a very special kind of design nirvana with a client who truly shares his or her sensibility. That's when the wonderful, if sometimes fraught work process becomes so positively joyous that you don't want it to end.

Such was the case here. This client and I match, perfectly. When it comes to palette and personality — and, I might add, wardrobe — we have an extraordinary affinity. We certainly share a taste for the theatrical when it comes to form, and neither one of us, clearly, is shy about our love of luster. The Seaman-Shepps Sputnik pulls on this orange-lacquer-finished chest of drawers, for example, are made of agate and studded with coral dots set in gold bezels.

You might think that we would egg each other on, and that the mix would spin out of control. Exactly the opposite happened. There's style and, I think, glamour, but no excess.

Putting things together is one of the trickiest parts of what any designer does. Editorial skills matter.

The mix comes from within, from the assuredness that, really, there are no rules. Yes, you can mix styles and periods and cultures.

The large chenille-covered, monogrammed, and befringed ottoman plays a central role in the marvelously personal mix of this room. I find that I use these oversize ottomans frequently because they can be used in a variety of ways — as a coffee table, for extra seating, or as a conversation starter.

The real pleasure of every room comes through a series of visual moments, which is why the mix is so important. I don't ever want anyone to be bored in a space that I've designed. I want my clients, and myself, to be able to sit in a room and keep discovering things — objects, materials, relationships between pattern, texture, and color. If the company is less than scintillating, guests, I hope, will entertain themselves by experiencing what's around them. The custom hand-painted screen lends additional color, and a lovely rusticity, to the corner behind the sofa. The glass lamp is Italian, from the 1950s.

There's nothing like a mythological reference to infuse even the most eclectic, personal mix with a spicy idiosyncracy. Two beautifully carved, exceptionally long-legged satyrs grace the frame of this nineteenth-century Italian settee. On the wall overhead are two paintings by Françoise Gillot; the third, smaller canvas is by the client's nephew. Although adorned with deep fringe and tassels, the curtains add a contemporary touch, thanks to the fact that they hang straight, without swoops or swags.

This marvelous French radiator cover dates to the Art Deco era. It adds a magnificent bit of whimsy and the suggestion of another window below the waist of the room. We inserted the blue frosted-glass panels and lit the whole thing from behind. The fish sculpture seems to underline the Françoise Gillot.

We have the unprecedented luxury of limitless opportunity: we can open ourselves to influences from around the world ...

Whatever American city we live in, we all inhabit a space filled with influences from our travels, the things we've acquired, and the experiences that have helped us grow.

An eighteenth-century scagliola tabletop features a border of mythical creatures and classical garlands around a central cartouche with an Italian scene. Mounted on a modern base carved and shaped in the traditional style, the decorative tabletop reiterates the arabesques of ornamentation that blossom elsewhere in the room. Atop the table is a Henry Moore sculpture, as well as a Chinese dish glazed in the classic Song Dynasty shade of celadon.

Afterword.

Design is magic, whether we care to admit it or not. Design, for me, is about beauty above all.

Like beauty, it has the power to bewitch. It can also transform and captivate and even educate. And while, again like beauty, it may be in the eye of the beholder — and thus defy any real, measurable, immutable definition — when it works it always casts the same sort of spell on those who are receptive to it. I happen to think that's all of us.

Beauty is what I hope to create for my clients, and what I insist on for myself and for my friends. I'm not, like Keats, obsessed with the equation of truth and beauty. But I absolutely understand the impulse to write an ode to a Grecian urn. After all, what could be more wonderful than to live with the carefully chosen object, the one the eye and the heart have prized? What could be more enchanting than the effect of that object in relation to other carefully chosen objects, each resonating with its own story and history? What could be more inspiring than to dwell among delicious textiles and fabulous materials, those many textures that delight the sense of touch? And what, ultimately, enthralls more than comfort? These are the things that make an environment glamorous, at least for me.

Luxury, glamour, and beauty — how deeply satisfying! A sense of luxury, after all, doesn't necessarily depend on gilt or satin or silk. Luxury, at least for a designer, is

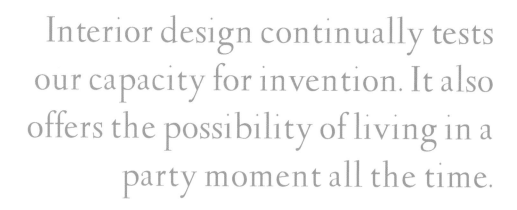

Interior design continually tests our capacity for invention. It also offers the possibility of living in a party moment all the time.

the opportunity to create spaces that reflect the personalities of those who dwell in them and that highlight their strengths and reveal something of their character. Gloss and glimmer, sheen and shimmer — these are the devices that I use to create the New American Glamour. But I could just as easily achieve my ends with other elements, such as the nubs of linen, say, or the softness of wool, or the patina of antique woods.

From a very early age, I knew that I was meant — that I was destined — to be a designer. I have always loved the special kind of excitement that comes with exploration and the joy that discovery engenders. I have always thrived in the quest for visual stimulation. To this day, these remain my very particular pleasures: the hunt, the treasure, the perfect juxtaposition are what intrigue me most.

Design is my life, and my hobby. I'm never happier than when roaming through antique shops, whether in New York City, Paris, or London, or prowling the souks of Morocco or discovering the weavers of Indonesia and combing through the marble yards of India. The challenge is always to find a way to bring all these things together. The solutions, I hope, express my vision of the New American Glamour.

I can't imagine anything more wonderful than spending my life sorting through civilizations and their contents. There are, after all, so many things to love. I don't think we should be limited by any one specific place or time because life itself is a series of endless possibilities and choices. Why say no to any of them?

Clockwise from top left: I treat my office as a canvas for my enthusiasms. Here a Moroccan table inlaid with mother-of-pearl sits atop a boldly patterned rug of my own design. Fabrics are a designer's most delicious and useful tool in terms of color, texture, and luster. Cut velvet, for example, always talks to the hand, which cannot help but touch. I personally love history, and I am fascinated by the elements of décor that have a long and storied past — such as animal prints, which have always been and will always be glamorous. For me, work is not a four-letter word. It's my life, and I love it. Why shouldn't my staff and I spend the day in a joyous, light-filled space surrounded by things of beauty?

Acknowledgments & Credits.

If I were to think that producing this book took nine months, I would be fooling myself. In fact, it has taken twenty-seven years, since my graduation from college, or maybe it has actually been even longer … my entire life. There are so many whom I wish to acknowledge:

172

At Bulfinch Press: Jill Cohen, fabulous champion and cheerleader, and Kristen Schilo, editor extraordinaire, for approaching me with this project and making it come alive.

Thank you to William Waldron, for your great photography and unerring eye; Judith Nasatir, for taking my mumbo-jumbo and crafting it into a vibrant text that truly captures my voice; Lisa Vaughn-Soraghan, whose sensitive design showcases my dramatic flair and whose grace is much appreciated.

I would like to thank each of the contributing photographers for beautifully documenting my work over the years: Michel Arnaud, John Bessler,

Bruce Buck, Pieter Estersohn, Elizabeth Felicella, Dennis Krukowski, Eric Laignel, John Edward Linden, Peter Mauss, Jon Miller, Minh + Wass, Edward J. North, Peter Peirce, Eric Striffler, Ben Stockley, Maria B. Sygman, Fritz Von Der Schulenburg, Wouter Vandertol, and Yale Wagner … in the end, it's all about the pictures.

In my office, there are so many who have contributed over the years. First, Susan Manne, whose hard work has benefited our clients and me for seventeen years. Thank you to the very stylish and talented Maryse Livoti, Mark Holmquist, and James Spodnik; and to David Spector, Jean-Luc Briguet and Dale Cohen, Melissa Smiley and Keith Shore for their efforts along the way.

Posthumously, I must remember my dear classmate from Parsons and early business partner, Felix Garkosky, and his lover and our business champion, Walter Porczak. Others whose style and influence stay with me to this day: Keith Bocash, Kevin Emard, and Len Nuvoloni. Also, early supporters and clients Alice Magdol Conrad and Elga Stulman, who opened so many doors and were such good friends — all gone but never forgotten.

I receive brilliant guidance from Steven Sonet, Esq., Gary Press, CPA, and Brendan Brennan. I am eternally grateful to Philip Hewat-Jaboor, to whom so many appreciations are due.

To the clients who gave me the opportunity and their confidence to create this work, not enough thanks can be extended.

Lastly, to Jason Witcher, without whose dedication, vision, and tenacity this book would never have come to fruition.

All photography not listed below is by William Waldron

Michel Arnaud: p. 21; John Bessler: pp. 22, 85 right; Photograph by Bruce Buck: p.111; Pieter Estersohn: pp. 134, 135; © 2003 Elizabeth Felicella Photography: pp. 122, 123; © Dennis Krukowski: pp. 3, 44, 45; Eric Laignel: pp. 6 top right, 24, 48, 169, 171 all; Photo: John Edward Linden: pp. 11, 46, 47; © Peter Mauss/Esto: pp. 58, 59 top and bottom, 68, 69, 70; Jon Miller: pp. 54 top and bottom, 55; Minh + Wass: pp. 1, 14, 23, 53, 65, 108 left; Photo by Edward J. North: pp. 42, 43, 158, 159, 160, 161; Photo © Peter Peirce: pp. 9, 56, 57, 109, 128, 130, 131, 154, 155; James Spodnik: p. 10; Ben Stockley: pp.18, 64; Eric Striffler: p. 17; Maria B. Sygman: pp. 28, 29, 52, 53, 80, 81, 120, 121, 144, 145, 172, 173; Photographer: Fritz Von Der Schulenburg: pp. 7 left, 146, 147, 148 top and bottom, 149, 150, 151, 167; Wouter Vandertol: p. 4; Photography © Yale Wagner: pp. 98, 99

Index.

174

Equally comfortable in traditional and contemporary styles, Jamie Drake has a gift for creating glamorous interiors that are inviting, fresh, and full of color. Since he launched Drake Design Associates in 1978, he has completed a vast array of residences, including a Los Angeles showplace for Madonna as well as multiple projects for New York City Mayor Michael Bloomberg, among them the renovation and restoration of Gracie Mansion. Drake's work has taken him to London, Paris, Bermuda, and the Middle East as well as throughout the United States.

Jamie Drake frequently participates in the country's most prestigious show houses: the Kips Bay Boys and Girls Club Decorator Show House, the Esquire Showhouse, the Junior League Showhouse, the Ebay Showhouse, the Hampton Designer Show House at Villa Maria, the French Designer Show House, and the Southampton Rogers Memorial Library Show House, among others. His work has often been published in *Architectural Digest,* French *Architectural Digest, Elle Décor,* and *House Beautiful,* as well as the *New York Times, House & Garden, Interior Design,* and *Metropolitan Home.* Once hailed by *Vanity Fair* as "a standout among the rising stars of interior designers," Drake has since been cited on the top interior designers lists of *House Beautiful, Gotham Magazine,* and *New York* magazine. In 2003, he was inducted into the Interior Design Hall of Fame and was named International Interior Designer of the Year.